PRAYERS
WITH ■ THE
DYING

LITURGY
TRAINING
PUBLICATIONS

Acknowledgments

Excerpts from the English translation of *Pastoral Care of the Sick: Rites of Anointing and Viaticum* © 1982, International Committee on English in the Liturgy, Inc. (ICEL); excerpts from the English translation of *A Book of Prayers* © 1982, ICEL; excerpt from the English translation of *Order of Christian Funerals* © 1985, ICEL; the English translation of the psalms from the *Liturgical Psalter* © 1994, ICEL. All rights reserved.

Scripture passages are taken from the New Revised Standard Version, copyright © 1989, Division of Christian Education, National Council of the Churches of Christ in the United States of America.

"Keep in Mind," by Lucien Deiss, copyright © 1965, World Library Publications, a division of J. S. Paluch Co., Inc. 3825 N. Willow Rd., Schiller Park, IL 60176. All rights reserved. Used by permission.

This book was compiled by David Philippart. Audrey Novak Riley was the production editor. It was designed by Anna Manhart and Kerry Perlmutter and typeset in Galliard by Karen Mitchell. Katharine Weingart-Wolff created the artwork. *Prayers with the Dying* was printed by Salsedo Press in Chicago, Illinois.

Copyright © 1997, Archdiocese of Chicago: Liturgy Training Publications, 1800 North Hermitage Avenue, Chicago IL 60622-1101; 1-800-933-1800; fax 1-800-933-7094; e-mail orders@ltp.org. All rights reserved.

Library of Congress Catalog Card Number: 97-69947

ISBN 1-56854-115-5

DYING

01 00 99 98 97   5 4 3 2 1

*Into your hands
I commend my spirit.*

*Dying you destroyed our death,
Rising you restored our life.
Lord Jesus,
come in Glory!*

The Hour Is Come: Watch and Pray

Gathered in this book are prayers and scriptures and songs to help you pray with a loved one who is dying. Use what is helpful here, and pay close attention to the words and images that surface from deep within your heart, too.

The first section, "Food for the Journey," offers a guide for celebrating the last sacrament, holy communion for the dying. Call your parish to arrange for this important rite. The next section, "Keeping Watch," is the heart of the book. It will help you keep watch at the bedside of your loved one. Included toward the end of this section are some short prayers and scripture verses that can be used in even the most trying situations. Sometimes taking a single short phrase and repeating it softly, over and over again, can help. Don't dismiss the suggestion of singing. If the songs provided do not help you, sing songs that you know by heart. Singing can give voice to the depths of sadness, kindle hope and soothe fear.

The third section, "At the Hour of Death," offers prayers for when death is imminent. Remember that even if a person is unconscious or unable to communicate, often she or he can still hear you. The final section, "Prayers after Death," is for use in the sad and numb moments immediately following death.

This is your loved one's passover. May God send holy angels to strengthen you in your waiting and watching, to comfort you in your sorrow and pain and to bring you peace.

Food for the Journey

When holy communion is shared with the dying, it is called "viaticum." This is a Latin word that means "food to go with you on the way." The bread of life, the cup of eternal salvation — these are our final nourishment in this life, and our promise of safe passover to the next. Jesus said that those who eat of this bread and drink of this cup have eternal life.

The most complete form of viaticum is to celebrate Mass at the bedside of the dying Christian. Since that is not always possible, communion can be brought from a celebration of Mass back at the parish church. The rite of communion of the dying is easy to follow, and it can be brief when necessary. It is best done with the participation of other parishioners, family members and friends, and even those caregivers present who may wish to join in. Depending on the condition of the dying Christian, there may be singing at the beginning and after communion (perhaps of songs that all know by heart). There will be a reading from scripture, prayers, including the Lord's Prayer, and times for silent reflection. Anyone who normally could receive communion at Mass is welcome to share in the eucharist at viaticum, too—a sure sign of our oneness in Christ, a love that is stronger than death.

The order of prayer is:

    Introductory Rites
        Greeting
        Sprinkling with Holy Water
        Instruction
        Penitential Rite

    Liturgy of the Word
        Reading
        Homily
        Baptismal Profession of Faith
        Litany

    Liturgy of Viaticum
        The Lord's Prayer
        Communion as Viaticum
        Silent Prayer
        Prayer after Communion

Concluding Rites
  Blessing
  Sign of Peace

To prepare for the celebration of viaticum, cover a table near the bed of the dying Christian with a cloth. You may light one or two candles (if you are at home and no oxygen tanks are present).

Find and mark in a Bible one of these passages:

  John 6:54–55
  John 14:23
  John 15:4
  1 Corinthians 11:26

Other passages, such as those on pages 18, 25 and 27, also may be used. Before beginning, ask someone to do the reading when the time comes.

We Prepare to Hear God's Word

The minister greets the one who is sick and all present.

All respond: **And also with you.**

Then the minister places the vessel containing the holy eucharist on a table, and all pause for a moment of silent adoration.

The minister, if a priest or deacon, may sprinkle all present with holy water, as a reminder of holy baptism.

Then the minister offers a brief instruction.

If the minister is a priest, the one who is sick may now celebrate the sacrament of penance. If so, others should withdraw a moment for privacy, and then the penitential rite is omitted.

The minister invites all present to ponder God's mercy.

Then all say:

I confess to almighty God,
and to you, my brothers and sisters,
that I have sinned through my own fault

All strike their breast.

in my thoughts and in my words,
in what I have done,
and in what I have failed to do;
and I ask blessed Mary, ever virgin,
all the angels and saints,
and you, my brothers and sisters,
to pray for me to the Lord our God.

Or the minister says:

By your paschal mystery you have won for us salvation: Lord, have mercy.
All: **Lord, have mercy.**

You renew among us now the wonders of your passion: Christ, have mercy.
All: **Christ, have mercy.**

When we receive your body, you share with us your paschal sacrifice: Lord, have mercy.
All: **Lord, have mercy.**

Then the minister concludes by invoking God's mercy and all reply: **Amen.**

If the minister is a priest, the apostolic pardon may be given now.

We Listen to God's Word

The reader reads the scripture that was marked in the Bible before we began.

If possible, a brief moment of silent reflection now follows, and the minister may offer some words about the scripture that we have just heard.

We Remember Baptism

The minister asks the one who is sick:

N., do you believe in God, the Father almighty,
creator of heaven and earth?
Response: **I do.**

Do you believe in Jesus Christ,
  his only Son, our Lord,
who was born of the Virgin Mary,
was crucified, died, and was buried,
rose from the dead,
and is now seated at the right hand
  of the Father?
Response: **I do.**

Do you believe in the Holy Spirit,
the holy catholic Church,
  the communion of saints,
the forgiveness of sins,
  the resurrection of the body,
and life everlasting?
Response: **I do.**

Then all respond to the invocations of the minister with the reply: **Lord, hear our prayer.**

WE SHARE THE BODY AND BLOOD OF CHRIST

The minister invites all to pray the Lord's Prayer. Then the minister shows the eucharist to all, who say:

Lord, I am not worthy to receive you, but only say the word and I shall be healed.

The minister offers the body of Christ and the blood of Christ to the one who is sick, and then says:

May the Lord Jesus Christ protect you
and lead you to eternal life.
Response: **Amen.**

Then others may receive communion.

A period of silence follows, or all may sing songs of praise if that seems appropriate. Use songs all know by heart, or see pages 17, 19, 23, 24 and 28.

The minister says a prayer, and all reply: **Amen.**

We Ask God's Blessing

A blessing is said, and after each invocation, all reply: **Amen.**

We Share a Sign of Peace

To conclude our prayer, we offer one another a sign of peace.

Keeping Watch

A New Heaven, A New Earth

Then I saw a new heaven and a new earth; for the first heaven and the first earth had passed away, and the sea was no more. And I saw the holy city, the new Jerusalem, coming down out of heaven from God, prepared as a bride adorned for her husband. And I heard a loud voice from the throne saying,

> "See, the home of God is among mortals.
> God will dwell with them as their God;
> they will be his peoples,
> and God himself will be with them;
> God will wipe every tear from their eyes.
> Death will be no more;
> mourning and crying and pain will be
>   no more,
> for the first things have passed away."

The one who was seated on the throne said, "See, I am making all things new. It is done! I am the Alpha and the Omega, the beginning and the end. To the thirsty, I will give water as a gift from the spring of the water of life. Those who conquer will inherit these things, and I will be their God and they will be my children."

—*Revelation 21:1–5a, 6–7*

Jerusalem, My Happy Home

This song can be sung to any common meter tune, such as LAND OF REST or "O God our help in ages past."

Jerusalem, my happy home,
When shall I with you be?
When shall my sorrows have an end?
Your joys when shall I see?

Your saints are crowned with glory great;
They see God face to face;
They triumph still; they still rejoice
In that most holy place.

Jerusalem, Jerusalem,
God grant that I may see
Your endless joy, and of the same
Partaker ever be!

—*Joseph Bromehead*

Pray for Me

Holy Mary, pray for me.

Saint Joseph, pray for me.

Jesus, Mary and Joseph,
assist me in my last agony.

Take This Cup

Jesus came out and went, as was his custom, to the Mount of Olives; and the disciples followed him. When he reached the place, he said to them, "Pray that you may not come into the time of trial." Then he withdrew from them about a stone's throw, knelt down, and prayed, "Father, if you are willing, remove this cup from me; yet not my will but yours be done." Then an angel from heaven appeared to him and gave him strength. In his anguish he prayed more earnestly, and his sweat became like great drops of blood falling down on the ground.

—*Luke 22:39–44*

From the Depths

From the depths I call to you,
Lord, hear my cry.
Catch the sound of my voice
raised up, pleading.

If you record our sins,
Lord, who could survive?
But because you forgive,
we stand in awe.

I trust in God's word,
I trust in the Lord.
More than sentries for dawn
I watch for the Lord.

More than sentries for dawn
let Israel watch.
The Lord will bring mercy
and grant full pardon.
The Lord will free Israel
from all its sins.

—*Psalm 130*

When from Death I'm Free

What wondrous love is this, O my soul?
What wondrous love is this, O my soul?
What wondrous love is this that caused
   the Lord of bliss
To bear the dreadful curse for my soul,
To bear the dreadful curse for my soul?

To God and to the Lamb, I will sing.
To God and to the Lamb, I will sing.
To God and to the Lamb, who is the great
   "I Am"
While millions join the theme, I will sing.
While millions join the theme, I will sing.

And when from death I'm free, I'll sing on.
And when from death I'm free, I'll sing on.
And when from death I'm free, I'll sing
   and joyful be,
And through eternity, I'll sing on.
And through eternity I'll sing on.

— *Alexander Means*

The Sun's Light Failed

It was now about noon, and darkness came over the whole land until three in the afternoon, while the sun's light failed; and the curtain in the temple was torn in two. Then Jesus, crying with a loud voice, said, "Father, into your hands I commend my spirit." Having said this, he breathed his last. When the centurion saw what had taken place, he praised God and said, "Certainly this man was innocent." And when all the crowds who had gathered for this spectacle saw what had taken place, they returned home, beating their breasts. But all his acquaintances, including the women who had followed him from Galilee, stood at a distance, watching these things.

—*Luke 23:44–49*

Why?

God, my God,
why have you abandoned me —
far from my cry, my words of pain?
I call by day, you do not answer;
I call by night, but find no rest.

Do not stay far off,
danger is so close.
I have no other help.

I am poured out like water,
my bones are pulled apart,
my heart is wax melting within me,
my throat baked and dry,
my tongue stuck to my jaws.
You bring me down to the dust of death.

Lord, do not stay far off,
you, my strength, be quick to help.

—*Psalm 22:1–3, 12, 15–16, 20*

Carry Me Home

Swing low, sweet chariot,
   coming for to carry me home!
Swing low, sweet chariot,
   coming for to carry me home!

> I looked over Jordan, and what did I see?
> Coming for to carry me home!
> A band of angels coming after me,
> Coming for to carry me home.
>
> If you get there before I do,
> Coming for to carry me home!
> Tell all my friends I'm coming, too.
> Coming for to carry me home.
>
> I'm sometimes up, I'm sometimes down.
> Coming for to carry me home!
> But still my soul feels heavenly bound.
> Coming for to carry me home.

—*African American spiritual*

Steal Away to Jesus

Steal away, steal away, steal away to Jesus!
Steal away, steal away home,
   I ain't got long to stay here.

My Lord, he calls me, he calls me
   by the thunder;
The trumpet sounds within my soul;
   I ain't got long to stay here.

Green trees are bending, poor sinners stand
   a-trembling;
The trumpet sounds within my soul;
   I ain't got long to stay here.

My Lord, he calls me, he calls me by the
   lightning;
The trumpet sounds within my soul;
   I ain't got long to stay here.

   —*African American spiritual*

Do Not Be Afraid

Jesus said, "Do not let your hearts be troubled. Believe in God, believe also in me. In my Father's house there are many dwelling places. If it were not so, would I have told you that I go to prepare a place for you? And if I go and prepare a place for you, I will come again and take you to myself, so that where I am, there you may be also. And you know the way to the place where I am going." Thomas said to him, "Lord, we do not know where you are going. How can we know the way?" Jesus said to him, "I am the way, and the truth, and the life. No one comes to the Father except through me."

"Those who love me will keep my word, and my Father will love them, and we will come to them and make our home with them."

"Peace I leave with you; my peace I give to you. I do not give to you as the world gives. Do not let your hearts be troubled, and do not let them be afraid."

—*John 14:1 – 6, 23, 27*

The Lord, My Shepherd

The Lord is my shepherd,
I need nothing more.
You give me rest in green meadows,
setting me near calm waters,
where you revive my spirit.

You guide me along sure paths,
you are true to your name.
Though I should walk in death's dark valley,
I fear no evil with you by my side,
your shepherd's staff to comfort me.

You spread a table before me
as my foes look on.
You soothe my head with oil;
my cup is more than full.

Goodness and love will tend me
every day of my life.
I will dwell in the house of the Lord
as long as I shall live.

—*Psalm 23*

On the Third Day Rise Again

On the first day of the week, at early dawn, the women came to the tomb, taking the spices they had prepared. They found the stone rolled away from the tomb, but when they went in they did not find the body. While they were perplexed about this, two men in dazzling clothes stood beside them. The women were terrified and bowed their faces to the ground, but the men said to them, "Why do you look for the living among the dead? He is not here, but has risen. Remember how he told you, while he was still in Galilee, that the Son of Man must be handed over to sinners, and be crucified, and on the third day rise again." Then they remembered his words, and returning from the tomb, they told all this to the eleven and all the rest. Now it was Mary Magdalene, Joanna, Mary the mother of James, and the other women with them who told this to the apostles.

—*Luke 24:1–11*

Freedom Is Coming!

Freedom is coming, freedom is coming!
Freedom is coming, O yes, I know.

> O yes, I know! O yes, I know!
> O yes, I know! O yes, I know!

Jesus is coming, Jesus is coming!
Jesus is coming, O yes, I know.

> O yes, I know! O yes, I know!
> O yes, I know! O yes, I know!

—*South African spiritual*

Saint Joseph, Pray for Us

Saint Joseph, pray for us!
Comfort of the troubled, pray for us!
Hope of the sick, pray for us!
Patron of the dying, pray for us!
Terror of evil spirits, pray for us!

Short Verses of Scripture

Pray one or more of these short texts with the one who is dying. If it helps to do so, softly repeat the phrase over and over as a mantra.

Who will separate us from the love of Christ?

—*Romans 8:35*

Whether we live or whether we die,
 we are the Lord's.

—*Romans 14:8*

If the earthly tent we live in is destroyed,
we have a building from God,
a house not made with hands,
eternal in the heavens.

—*2 Corinthians 5:1*

We will see God as God is.

—*1 John 3:2*

We know that we have passed
   from death to life
because we love each other.

   —*1 John 3:14*

Though I should walk
   in death's dark valley,
I fear no evil with you by my side.

   —*Psalm 23:4*

Lord, I give myself to you.

   —*Psalm 25:1*

The Lord is my saving light.

   —*Psalm 27:1*

I know I will see
how good God is
while I am still alive.

   —*Psalm 27:13*

I put myself in your hands,
knowing you will save me.

— *Psalm 31:6*

I thirst for God,
the living God.

— *Psalm 42:3*

Come, you that are blessed by my Father,
says the Lord Jesus,
inherit the kingdom prepared for you
from the foundation of the world.

— *Matthew 25:34*

The Lord Jesus says,
Today you will be with me in paradise.

— *Luke 23:43*

I will raise them up on the last day,
says the Lord Jesus.

— *John 6:40*

In my Father's house
there are many dwelling places,
says the Lord Jesus.

   —*John 14:2*

The Lord Jesus says,
I go and prepare a place for you,
I will come again and will take you to myself.

   —*John 14:3*

I desire that those you have given me
may be with me where I am,
says the Lord Jesus.

   —*John 17:24*

Lord Jesus, receive my spirit.

   —*Acts 7:59*

Litany of the Saints

When the condition of the dying person calls for the use of brief forms of prayer, those who are present are encouraged to pray the litany of the saints—or at least some of its invocations—for him or her. Special mention may be made of the patron saints of the dying person, of the family and of the parish. The litany may be said or sung in the usual way.

Lord, have mercy	**Lord, have mercy**
Christ, have mercy	**Christ, have mercy**
Lord, have mercy	**Lord, have mercy**
Holy Mary, Mother of God	**Pray for *him/her***
Holy angels of God	**Pray for *him/her***
Abraham, our father in faith	**Pray for *him/her***
Sarah, our mother in faith	**Pray for *him/her***
David, leader of God's people	**Pray for *him/her***

All holy patriarchs, matriarchs and prophets	**Pray for *him/her***
Saint John the Baptist	**Pray for *him/her***
Saint Joseph	**Pray for *him/her***
Saint Peter and Saint Paul	**Pray for *him/her***
Saint Andrew	**Pray for *him/her***
Saint John	**Pray for *him/her***
Saint Mary Magdalene	**Pray for *him/her***
Saint Stephen	**Pray for *him/her***
Saint Ignatius	**Pray for *him/her***
Saint Lawrence	**Pray for *him/her***
Saint Perpetua and Saint Felicity	**Pray for *him/her***
Saint Agnes	**Pray for *him/her***
Saint Gregory	**Pray for *him/her***
Saint Monica	**Pray for *him/her***

Saint Augustine	**Pray for** *him/her*
Saint Athanasius	**Pray for** *him/her*
Saint Basil	**Pray for** *him/her*
Saint Macrina	**Pray for** *him/her*
Saint Martin	**Pray for** *him/her*
Saint Benedict	**Pray for** *him/her*
Saint Scholastica	**Pray for** *him/her*
Saint Francis and Saint Dominic	**Pray for** *him/her*
Saint Clare	**Pray for** *him/her*
Saint Patrick	**Pray for** *him/her*
Saint Bridget	**Pray for** *him/her*
Saint Thomas More	**Pray for** *him/her*
Saint Catherine	**Pray for** *him/her*
Saint Teresa	**Pray for** *him/her*
Saint Charles Lwanga	**Pray for** *him/her*

Saint Stanislaus	**Pray for** *him/her*
Saint Ludmilla	**Pray for** *him/her*
Saint Chong Hasong	**Pray for** *him/her*
Saint Andrew Kim	**Pray for** *him/her*
Saint Martin de Porres	**Pray for** *him/her*
Saint Rose of Lima	**Pray for** *him/her*
Saint Frances Cabrini	**Pray for** *him/her*
Saint John Neumann	**Pray for** *him/her*
Saint Elizabeth Ann Seton	**Pray for** *him/her*

Other saints may be included here.

All holy men and women	**Pray for** *him/her*
Lord, be merciful	**Lord, save your people**
From all evil	**Lord, save your people**
From every sin	**Lord, save your people**
From Satan's power	**Lord, save your people**

At the moment of death	**Lord, save your people**
From everlasting death	**Lord, save your people**
On the day of judgment	**Lord, save your people**
By your coming as one of us	**Lord, save your people**
By your suffering and cross	**Lord, save your people**
By your death and rising to new life	**Lord, save your people**
By your return in glory to the Father	**Lord, save your people**
By your gift of the Holy Spirit	**Lord, save your people**
By your coming again in glory	**Lord, save your people**

Be merciful to us sinners	**Lord, hear our prayer**
Bring *N.* to eternal life, first promised to *him/her* in baptism	**Lord, hear our prayer**
Raise *N.* on the last day, for *he/she* has eaten the bread of life	**Lord, hear our prayer**
Let *N.* share in your glory, for *he/she* has shared in your suffering and death	**Lord, hear our prayer**
Jesus, Son of the living God	**Lord, hear our prayer**
Christ, hear us	**Christ, hear us**
Lord Jesus, hear our prayer	**Lord Jesus, hear our prayer.**

At the Hour of Death

Now and at the Hour

Hail Mary, full of grace,
the Lord is with you!
Blessed are you among women
and blessed is the fruit of your womb, Jesus.
Holy Mary, Mother of God,
pray for us sinners
now and at the hour of our death. Amen.

Go Forth

Go forth, Christian soul, from this world
in the name of God the almighty Father,
who created you,
in the name of Jesus Christ,
   Son of the living God,
who suffered for you,
in the name of the Holy Spirit,
who was poured out upon you,
go forth, faithful Christian.

May you live in peace this day,
may your home be with God in Zion,

with Mary, the virgin Mother of God,
with Joseph, and all the angels and saints.

— *Pastoral Care of the Sick*

May You Return to God

I commend you, my dear *brother/sister*,
   to almighty God,
and entrust you to your Creator.
May you return to the One
who formed you from the dust of the earth.
May holy Mary, the angels, and all the saints
come to meet you as you go forth from this life.
May Christ who was crucified for you
bring you freedom and peace.
May Christ who died for you
admit you into his garden of paradise.
May Christ, the true Shepherd,
acknowledge you as one of his flock.
May he forgive all your sins,
and set you among those he has chosen.
May you see your Redeemer face to face,
and enjoy the vision of God for ever. Amen.

— *Pastoral Care of the Sick*

Keep in Mind

Keep in mind that Jesus Christ has died for us
   and is risen from the dead.
He is our saving Lord.
He is joy for all ages.

> If we die with the Lord, we shall live
>   with the Lord.
> If we endure with the Lord, we shall reign
>   with the Lord.

In him all our sorrow, in him all our joy.

In him hope of glory, in him all our love.

In him our redemption, in him all our grace.

In him our salvation, in him all our peace.

—*Lucien Deiss*

I Shall See God

Job said, "I know that my Redeemer lives, and that at the last, he will stand upon the earth; and after my skin has been thus destroyed, then in my flesh I shall see God, whom I shall see on my side, and my eyes shall behold, and not another."

—*Job 19:25–27a*

Deliver Your Servant, Lord

One person says the invocation, and all respond.

Welcome your servant, Lord, into the place of
 salvation, which, because of your mercy,
 he/she rightly hoped for.
Lord, save your people. *or* **Amen.**

Deliver your servant, Lord,
 from every distress.
Lord, save your people. *or* **Amen.**

Deliver your servant, Lord, as you delivered
Noah from the flood.
Lord, save your people. *or* **Amen.**

Deliver your servant, Lord, as you delivered
Abraham from Ur of the Chaldees.
Lord, save your people. *or* **Amen.**

Deliver your servant, Lord, as you delivered
Moses from the hand of the Pharaoh.
Lord, save your people. *or* **Amen.**

Deliver your servant, Lord, as you delivered
Daniel from the den of lions.
Lord, save your people. *or* **Amen.**

Deliver your servant, Lord, as you delivered
the three youths from the fiery furnace.
Lord, save your people. *or* **Amen.**

Deliver your servant, Lord, as you delivered
Susanna from her false accusers.
Lord, save your people. *or* **Amen.**

Deliver your servant, Lord, as you delivered
	David from the attacks of Saul and Goliath.
Lord, save your people. *or* **Amen.**

Deliver your servant, Lord, as you delivered
	Peter and Paul from prison.
Lord, save your people. *or* **Amen.**

Deliver your servant, Lord,
	through Jesus our Savior,
who suffered death for us
	and gave us eternal life.
Lord, save your people. *or* **Amen.**

—*Pastoral Care of the Sick*

Savior of the World

Lord Jesus Christ, Savior of the world,
we pray for your servant, *N.,*
and commend *him/her* to your mercy.
For *his/her* sake you came down from heaven;
receive *him/her* now
	into the joy of your kingdom.

For though *he/she* has sinned,
he/she has not denied the Father, the Son,
   and the Holy Spirit,
but has believed in God
and has worshiped *his/her* Creator.
Amen.

—*Pastoral Care of the Sick*

Salve Regina

Hail, holy Queen, Mother of mercy,
hail, our life, our sweetness, and our hope.
To you we cry, the children of Eve;
to you we send up our sighs,
mourning and weeping in this land of exile.
Turn, then, most gracious advocate,
your eyes of mercy toward us;
lead us home at last
and show us the blessed fruit
   of your womb, Jesus:
O clement, O loving, O sweet Virgin Mary.

Prayers after Death

Saints of God

One person says the invocation, and all respond.

Saints of God, come to *his/her* aid!
Come to meet *him/her*, angels of the Lord!

**Receive *his/her* soul and present *him/her*
to God the Most High.**

May Christ, who called you, take you to himself;
may angels lead you to Abraham's side.

**Receive *his/her* soul and present *him/her*
to God the Most High.**

Give *him/her* eternal rest, O Lord,
and may your light shine on *him/her* forever.

**Receive *his/her* soul and present *him/her*
to God the Most High.**

Let us pray.

All-powerful and merciful God,
we commend to you *N.*, your servant.
In your mercy and love,

blot out the sins *he/she* has committed
   through human weakness.
In this world *he/she* has died:
let *him/her* live with you forever.

We ask this through Christ our Lord.
Amen.

— *Pastoral Care of the Sick*

Of Our Destiny

God of our destiny,
into your hands we commend our *brother/sister*.
We are confident that
   with all who have died in Christ
he/she will be raised to life on the last day
and live with Christ for ever.
We thank you for all the blessings
you gave *him/her* in this life
to show your fatherly care for all of us
and for the fellowship
   which is ours with the saints
in Jesus Christ.

Lord, hear our prayer:
welcome our *brother/sister* to paradise
and help us to comfort each other
with the assurance of our faith
until we all meet in Christ
to be with you and with our *brother/sister* for ever.
We ask this through Christ our Lord.
Amen.

— *Pastoral Care of the Sick*

A Brief Rite

This brief order of prayer may be used after a loved one has died, especially when ministers from the parish make their first visit. Before beginning, find and mark in your Bible one of these scripture passages:

Matthew 18:19–20
John 11:21–24
Luke 20:35–38

Other passages, such as those on page 21, 25 or 27 also may be used. The church's ritual book,

Order of Christian Funerals, gives more scripture suggestions. Choose someone to read the scripture at the appropriate time below.

The order of prayer is:

> Invitation to Prayer
> Reading
> The Lord's Prayer
> Prayer for the Deceased Person
> Prayer for the Mourners
> Blessing

We Are Invited to Pray

The minister or leader invites us to pray in these or similar words:

In this moment of sorrow
the Lord is in our midst
and consoles us with his word:
Blessed are the sorrowful;
   they shall be comforted.

We Listen to God's Word

The reader reads the scripture chosen before we began. We all pause for a moment to reflect on the scripture.

We Pray the Lord's Prayer

The minister or leader invites us to pray in the words Jesus taught us.

We Pray for the One Who Has Just Died

The minister or leader offers a prayer for the deceased, such as those on pages 55 through 58. We all respond: **Amen.**

We Pray for the Mourners

The minister or leader offers a prayer for the mourners, such as the one on page 59. We all respond: **Amen.**

We Ask God's Blessing

Minister or leader:

Blessed are those that have died in the Lord;
let them rest from their labors
   for their good deeds go with them.

All may sign the deceased on the forehead with the sign of the cross as the following prayer is said.

Minister or leader:

Eternal rest grant unto *him/her*, O Lord.

All: **And let perpetual light shine upon *him/her*.**

Minister or leader:

May *he/she* rest in peace.

All: **Amen.**

Minister or leader:

May *his/her* soul and the souls
 of all the faithful departed,
through the mercy of God, rest in peace.

All: **Amen.**

*The minister, if a priest or deacon, gives a blessing.
A lay minister or leader says:*

May the love of God and the peace
 of the Lord Jesus Christ
bless and console us
and gently wipe every tear from our eyes:
in the name of the Father,
and of the Son, and of the Holy Spirit.

All: **Amen.**

For the One Who Has Died

Holy Lord, almighty and eternal God,
hear our prayers for your servant *N.,*
whom you have summoned out of this world.
Forgive *him/her* sins and failings
and grant *him/her* a place of refreshment,
  light and peace.
Let *him/her* pass unharmed through
  the gates of death
to dwell with the blessed in light,
as you promised to Abraham
  and his children for ever.
Accept *N.* into your safekeeping
and on the great day of judgment
raise *him/her* up with all the saints
to inherit your eternal kingdom.

We ask this through Christ our Lord.
Amen.

  —*Order of Christian Funerals*

For the One Who Has Died

Into your hands, O Lord,
we humbly entrust our *brother/sister* N.
In this life you embraced *him/her*
    with your tender love;
deliver *him/her* now from every evil
and bid *him/her* enter eternal rest.

The old order has passed away:
welcome *him/her* then into paradise,
where there will be no sorrow,
    no weeping nor pain,
but the fullness of peace and joy
with your Son and the Holy Spirit
for ever and ever.
Amen.

    — *Order of Christian Funerals*

For One Who Died after a Long Illness

Most faithful God,
lively is the courage of those who hope in you.
Your servant *N.* suffered greatly
but placed *his/her* trust in your mercy.
Confident that the petition
　of those who mourn
pierces the clouds and finds an answer,
we beg you, give rest to *N.*
Do not remember *his/her* sins
but look upon *his/her* sufferings
and grant *him/her* refreshment, light, and peace.

We ask this through Christ our Lord.
Amen.

　—*Order of Christian Funerals*

For an Elderly Person

God of mercy,
look kindly on your servant *N.*
who has set down the burden of *his/her* years.
As *he/she* served you faithfully
  throughout *his/her* life,
may you give *him/her* the fullness
  of your peace and joy.
We give thanks for the long life of *N.*
now caught up in your eternal love.
We make our prayer in the name of Jesus
  who is our risen Lord now and for ever.
Amen.

—*Order of Christian Funerals*

For Those Who Mourn

Father of mercies and God of all consolation,
you pursue us with untiring love
and dispel the shadow of death
with the bright dawn of life.

Comfort your family in their loss and sorrow.
Be our refuge and our strength, O Lord,
and lift us from the depths of grief
into the peace and light of your presence.

Your Son, our Lord Jesus Christ,
by dying has destroyed our death,
and by rising, restored our life.
Enable us therefore to press on toward him,
so that, after our earthly course is run,
he may reunite us with those we love,
when every tear will be wiped away.

We ask this through Christ our Lord.
Amen.

—*Order of Christian Funerals*

Respect and Honor

Since in baptism the body was marked with the seal of the Trinity and became the temple of the Holy Spirit, Christians respect and honor the bodies of the dead and the places where they rest. Any customs associated with the preparation of the body of the deceased should always be marked with dignity and reverence and never with the despair of those who have no hope. Preparation of the body should include prayer, especially at those intimate moments reserved for family members. For the final disposition of the body, it is the ancient Christian custom to bury or entomb the bodies of the dead; cremation is permitted, unless it is evident that cremation was chosen for anti-Christian motives.

In countries or regions where an undertaker, and not the family or community, carries out the preparation and transfer of the body, the pastor and other ministers are to ensure that the undertakers appreciate the values and beliefs of the Christian community.

The family and friends of the deceased should not be excluded from taking part in the services sometimes provided by undertakers, for example, the preparation and laying out of the body.

—*Order of Christian Funerals*